AF255353

I HAVE A VOICE

A Children's Book About Advocacy in Healthcare

Author Seema Al-Hiraki
Illustrator Anna McDonald

"Chloe and Carter," called the doctor, "it's your turn."
"Yay," shouted Chloe.

They both rushed ahead of Mom into the doctor's room. Carter and Chloe were always excited to visit the doctor, because they learned so much.

"I see you're all grown up now!" said the doctor, looking at the twins.
"How are you today?" she asked.
The twins were silent. They felt nervous about answering the doctor.

As Carter looked around the room, he noticed a poster on the wall. It had the words **_Health Advocate_** on it.

Carter, a curious boy who was always eager to learn, pointed to the sign and asked, "Mom, what does that mean?"

Both the twins' mom and the doctor were happy to answer his question and teach Carter and Chloe all about advocacy *(ad-vo-ca-see)* in healthcare.

"Advocacy is when you help support and care for yourself or others," said Mom.

HEALTH ADVOCATE

The doctor nodded and added, "and advocacy in healthcare means to learn and teach rules that help your medical safety and the safety of others, and to always fight for the right thing to do."

"I don't understand," said Chloe, scrunching her nose up, "can you tell us more?"

"Hmmm," said Mom, thinking.
"Maybe we should give you some examples."

"For instance," said the doctor, "one way to be a health advocate is to not be afraid to speak up and ask questions."

"It helps you be ready for your doctor's visits," Mom pointed out, "because you'll be ready to answer any questions your doctor asks, big or small!"

"Plus, you can learn all about diseases and medications and teach others to help them too!" said the doctor.

"Wow, I want to do that when I grow up!" said Carter, his eyes wide.

"Me too!" exclaimed Chloe.

"Actually, you can start doing it right now!" said Mom.

"You can answer the question your doctor asked you today, and you can help each other when she asks you more questions!" said Mom.

"Yes, you can!" said the doctor. "Start today and when you grow up, you can also become a doctor like me and advocate for all your patients – doctors do that too! Are you ready to try?"

The twins shyly nodded their heads.

"How are you today?" the doctor asked with a twinkle in her eye.

"I'm good and I'm ready for my check up!" said Chloe.

"I'm good too," replied Carter.

Just then, Chloe remembered that Carter had fallen the day before, and she thought he should tell the doctor.

She looked at Carter, held his hand, and said, "Carter, don't be shy to speak up and tell the doctor how you are feeling after what happened yesterday."

Carter smiled and thanked Chloe, then told the doctor, "I fell on my foot yesterday when I was playing with Chloe. It hurts a little, but I was strong."

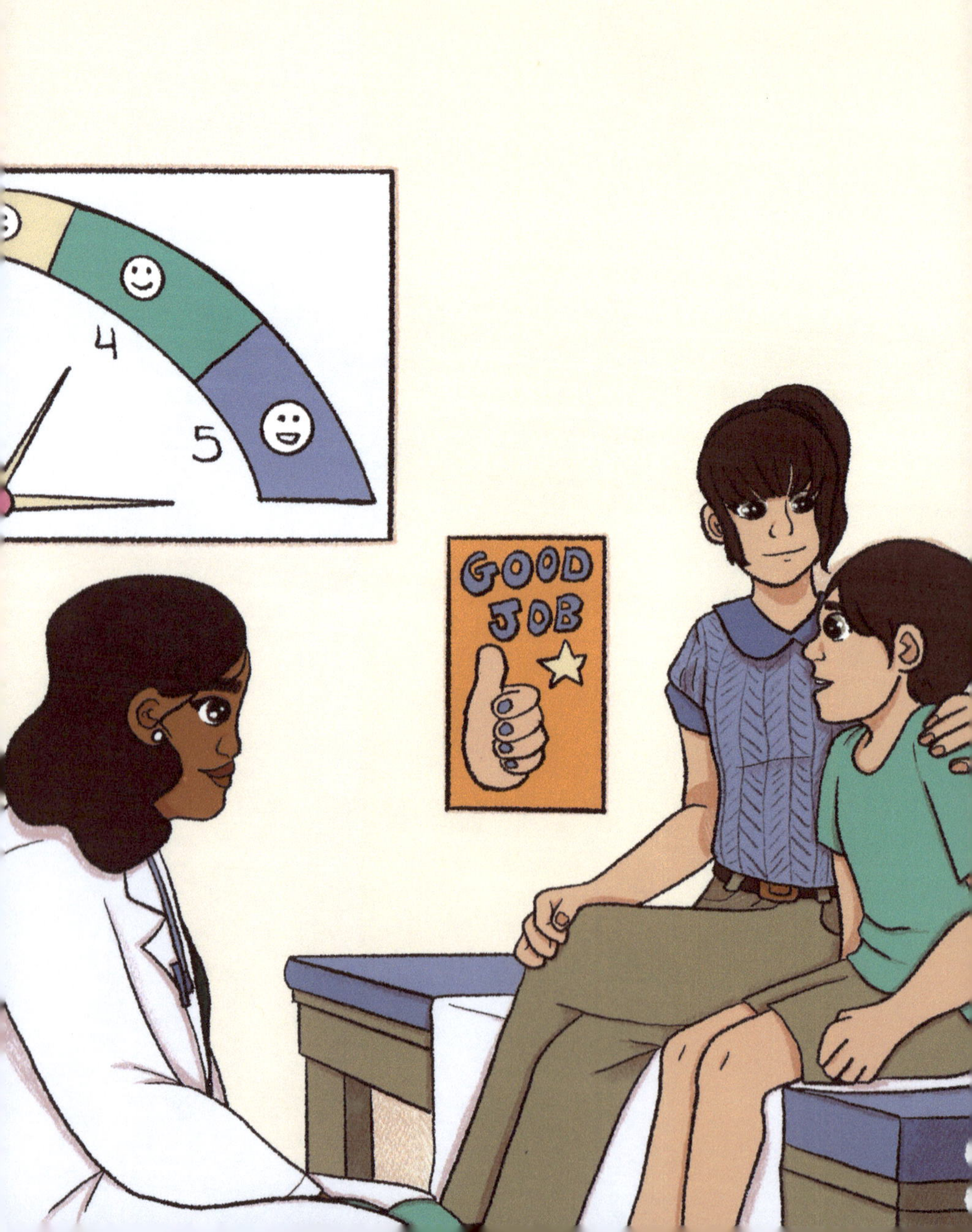
4
5
GOOD
JOB

Mom and the doctor were very proud of Carter for sharing that, and they were also proud of Chloe for being an advocate for herself and for Carter.

"Thank you for speaking up and for being strong," said the doctor. "I will take a look at your foot right away!" she smiled at Carter.

After the doctor finished their check ups, she explained all the good results and waited for any follow up questions.

When they were done, she gave thcm toys to take home and she said, "Thank you for being such good health advocates! See you in a few months for your next check up!"

"Thank you so much!" said the twins as they waved goodbye.

"What did you learn today, kids?" asked Mom.

"I learned what health advocacy means, why it's important, and how I can do it," said Carter.

"And I learned that I have a voice and I will use it," Chloe said confidently.

About The Author

Seema is a published author who completed her undergraduate studies in health sciences, biology and psychology at Purdue University and completed her graduate studies in physiology and biophysics at Georgetown University. Seema is pursuing a career in medicine and believes in the importance of advocacy, specifically within healthcare, and teaching it at such a young age. Seema's goal with this book is to simplify the concept of advocacy in healthcare for children to grasp and implement in their daily lives. She aims to continuously promote activism in an educational yet enjoyable way.